This journal belongs to

_____

Choose ♥ Love

A Mother's Blessing

GRATITUDE
JOURNAL

BELLE
★ CITY ★
GIFTS

Belle City Gifts
Racine, Wisconsin, USA

Belle City Gifts is an imprint of BroadStreet Publishing Group LLC.
Broadstreetpublishing.com

Choose Love

ISBN 978-1-4245-5087-6

Design by Garborg Design Works | www.garborgdesign.com
Editorial services by Michelle Winger | www.literallyprecise.com

Printed in China.

15   16   17   18   19   20   21   7   6   5   4   3   2   1

Introduction

Expressing love is at the very core of my life. I want my husband, my children, my family, my friends, and my community of blog readers to know that I love and appreciate them all in different but significant ways.

Now, just because intentionally choosing to express my love and affection for others is important to me doesn't mean that I do it perfectly or that I do it as consistently as I would like! Busyness can creep in, bad attitudes can fester, conflict can remain unresolved—all of these can prevent me from consciously and intentionally choosing to love someone else.

Last year, I released a *Choose Gratitude* journal, and was blown away by the response and excitement over it. This journal encouraged women to take just a few minutes each day to jot down a line or two of things they were grateful for. A year later, I continue to receive amazing stories from women whose lives have been transformed by the simple practice of going throughout their day looking for blessings.

My motivation in writing the *Choose Love* journal is similar. I want to focus my own heart on choosing love, even when my attitude or the circumstances make it difficult to do so. Rather than choosing to be angry or frustrated with daily interruptions, I want to choose love. Rather than choosing defeat or believing lies about who I am, I want to choose love. Rather than being consumed with the anxiety of hamster-wheel busyness, I want to choose love and a simpler lifestyle.

I have so much in my own life to be grateful for, and so many wonderful people to love. I want to be diligent about recording the blessings in my life and the many opportunities I have to love those dear to me, and I want to encourage you to do the same.

Choose love today!

Crystal Paine

January

*Choose love
with intention*

If you want to make
a difference in your
lifetime, daily goal-
setting is a tool to a
life well-lived.

*D*o you take time to ask questions with your friends? Real questions? Not the "how are you" and "how's the weather" kind of questions, but the kind of questions that cause people to be real and honest with where they are.

Recently I was with a friend, and I asked how she was doing. When she responded, "Okay," I looked at her and said, "You're not doing well, are you? What's going on?" This let her know that I really cared and wanted to know how she was. It gave her permission to share a struggle she was going through.

1. _____

2. _____

3. _____

4. _____

5. _____

6. _____

7. _____

Years that are composed of days spent with purpose and focus add up to a lifetime that has made a mark on this world.

What goals have you set for yourself this year?

Without goals you have no real purpose for going through your days.

8. _____

9. _____

10. _____

11. _____

12. _____

13. _____

14. _____

If you're aiming at nothing, you're not
going to feel inspired, motivated or driven.

What goals would you like to work on in the future:
relationally, professionally, physically, financially?

Goals give you momentum, passion for life,
and a reason to wake up every morning
excited about what lies ahead of you.

15. _____

16. _____

17. _____

18. _____

19. _____

20. _____

21. _____

You'll probably be amazed at how much more zest for life you'll have when you actually have a destination in mind and a plan to get there.

Is there an area you feel like you are floundering in, where some intentionality might be needed to get out of the rut?

You just might find that your renewed zeal helps you attack life with more energy and excitement.

22. _____

23. _____

24. _____

25. _____

26. _____

27. _____

28. _____

Choose to be intentional and purposeful in how you live, so that you make the most of all that you've been given instead of wishing you were someone else.

29. _____

30. _____

31. _____

Write down two specific, actionable things that you can
accomplish this week that will help repair a relationship,
rebuild trust, or show someone love.

love is dropping everything
to help someone else out.

February

Choose love in your close relationships

A good relationship is built

around humility and the

ability to say, "I was wrong.

Will you forgive me?"

These are hard words to

say, but they are necessary.

*H*ave you ever noticed how we often treat those closest to us the worst? We save our best manners for co-workers, acquaintances, and even strangers, while those in our own family will sometimes bear the brunt of our bad attitudes and irritable responses.

I know that some of this is because I feel most comfortable with those closest to me, but I've realized more and more that this is incredibly counter-productive to building the strong, loving relationships I need with the people who know me best. Slowly, God has started chipping away at my heart in this area.

Recently, I've made a conscious decision to praise and thank those closest to me for all the joy and strength they bring to my life. As a result, my most important relationships are becoming my strongest relationships because I'm actually taking the time and making the effort to show them just how much I love and appreciate them.

1. _____

2. _____

3. _____

4. _____

5. _____

6. _____

7. _____

A good friendship doesn't just happen;
it requires a lot of work and time and effort.

What are three simple things you can do this week to show love to those closest to you?

Just like you can't expect to build a muscular body without putting in a lot of time weight-lifting, you can't expect to have a strong relationship if you're not constantly building it up.

8. _____

9. _____

10. _____

11. _____

12. _____

13. _____

14. _____

Look for ways to show your appreciation
to your loved ones.

How do you typically respond to your close friends and
family when expectations are not met?

Think about how much effort you used
to put into your close relationships
to make them strong. Are you still
putting in enough work?

15. _____

16. _____

17. _____

18. _____

19. _____

20. _____

21. _____

There are always, always, always
good things to praise.

Is it easy to praise those close to you,

or do you find it to be a struggle?

Become someone who notices good
in your friends and family.

22. _____

23. _____

24. _____

25. _____

26. _____

27. _____

28. _____

Go throughout your day looking for ways
to build up, encourage, and love others.

What three things can you think of right now
that you can praise in your close relationships?

If you're too busy to invest
in your close relationships,
you're just plain too busy.

March

*Choose love
when it is hard*

No matter how hard life is right
now, remember that no one can
take away your ability to choose
your attitude in the middle of
difficult circumstances. Choose love.

*F*orgiveness is a choice we can make regardless of whether the other party asks for it or admits they were wrong. It's never an easy choice, but it's always the right choice. Recently, I was hurt by a long-time acquaintance. Even though I was angry about the situation, I wanted to choose forgiveness. I started refusing to allow upset thoughts to fester in my mind. Instead, I chose to pray for the woman and continually ask God to help me forgive her. Amazingly enough, as I changed my attitude toward the situation, I started to really love the woman and was able to overlook what she had done. Forgiveness is so much better than bitterness!

1. _____

2. _____

3. _____

4. _____

5. _____

6. _____

7. _____

Stay calm. Love, love, love. Don't lash out.

How do you normally face trials:

with a calm spirit or an anxious heart?

You can't always change your circumstances, but you can always choose your attitude. Choose love.

8. _____

9. _____

10. _____

11. _____

12. _____

13. _____

14. _____

Moms can get so busy with life. We have places to go, things to do, messes to clean up, and meals to fix. But our kids don't need our productivity. They need our presence.

What is one way you can ward off the pull to busyness this week and instead remain "present" with your children?

There is always something to be thankful for. Have the eyes to see it.

15. _____

16. _____

17. _____

18. _____

19. _____

20. _____

21. _____

Forgiveness is a choice.

What unexpected circumstances did you encounter
this week when you were tempted to lash out?

love isn't just a feeling.

22. _____

23. _____

24. _____

25. _____

26. _____

27. _____

28. _____

Love is giving up plans and being
available when someone else needs you.

29. _____

30. _____

31. _____

Name one thing that happened recently that
seemed very difficult at the time, but now you
are beginning to see it differently.

*love isn't just words
you say or write.*

April

Choose love in friendships

A good friendship
requires effort. It
doesn't just happen.
It means that both
parties make sacrifices
for each other.

Strong friendships don't just happen; they are the result of lots of nurturing and cultivating. They are borne out of the investment of time, resources, and energy. As a Type-A Driver personality who is also introverted, I can make productivity paramount to everything. But long term, this isn't healthy; it's also a sure-fire way to ruin relationships.

I'm learning that strong relationships require being willing to sacrifice and go outside my comfort zone to bless someone else. It's not always convenient, but it's always worth it.

There are so many blessings in living your life with outstretched arms.

1. _____

2. _____

3. _____

4. _____

5. _____

6. _____

7. _____

If you want authentic relationships, you first
have to be willing to be authentic yourself.

Do you have close, loving friendships right now, or do you see this as an area in which you need to invest and grow?

Stop hiding behind a fake, people-pleasing persona and start being genuinely you.

8. _____

9. _____

10. _____

11. _____

12. _____

13. _____

14. _____

Stop trying to please people; stop staying
closed up in an attempt to avoid getting hurt.

Have you been hurt in a past friendship?

Have you forgiven this person so that you can move on?

Start reaching out.
Be authentic.
Be 100 percent YOU.

15. _____

16. _____

17. _____

18. _____

19. _____

20. _____

21. _____

True friendships require commitment.

Is it easy for you to be authentic in your friendships?

True friends believe the best, speak the truth when needed, and don't gossip or slander.

22. _____

23. _____

24. _____

25. _____

26. _____

27. _____

28. _____

Friendship means you are *for* the other person.

29. _____

30. _____

What two character traits would you like to develop

in order to become a better friend?

As a true friend, you want others to succeed. You celebrate them. You appreciate them.

May

Choose love by giving

Focus on blessing others
and you'll often be
richly blessed in return.

*W*e aren't all passionate about the same causes. We aren't all supposed to invest in the same projects. But we should all invest in something and in someone in some place— whether that's in Haiti or New Hampshire or Africa or Arkansas. Whether that's in your own home, down the street, across the country, or around the world. We *all* have something to offer, something to give, and someone who needs what we have. Look around you and you'll see many needs. You can't meet them all. You aren't *supposed* to meet them all. But you can do what you can, with what you have, where you are. You can take what time and energy and skills you have and use them to bless *someone* in *some* way.

1. _____

2. _____

3. _____

4. _____

5. _____

6. _____

7. _____

People feel valued when you look them in the eyes
and genuinely listen to what they have to share.

Do you consider yourself a naturally giving person?

Give someone your undivided attention, and see what it does for them.

8. _____

9. _____

10. _____

11. _____

12. _____

13. _____

14. _____

Ask someone how you can be a better friend.

Their answer might truly surprise you.

If you feel like you tend to give, give, give in all of your relationships, have you found some resentment creeping in?

Knowing others' love languages is a tremendous help when it comes to relationships.

15. _____

16. _____

17. _____

18. _____

19. _____

20. _____

21. _____

Find out how you can love best. Is it words of
affirmation, a letter, a gift, an act of service?

Was there a time this week when you decided to choose love, even when you had nothing left to give?

It's easy to give from our abundance; true giving requires sacrifice.

22. _____

23. _____

24. _____

25. _____

26. _____

27. _____

28. _____

If you are thinking of someone,
let them know you're thinking of them.

29. _____

30. _____

31. _____

What simple action can you take today

to show someone you love them?

love is action. It is doing
and giving and serving.

June

*Choose love
when it hurts*

I want to live my life
with arms wide open:
willingly and gladly
giving of my best
for others, holding
nothing back.

Some of you are hurting right now. Despite how

someone else has made you feel, despite what the

voices in your head are telling you, you are not a failure.

You may have failed in some areas, but falling down

and making mistakes does not make you a failure. It just

means that you are human. You have worth. You have

immense value. Do not believe the lies that others (or

your own head) tell you, saying you are worthless or

good for nothing.

You have a story. You have unique life experience. You

have gifts and talents. You are the only *you*. The world

needs your gifts, your talents, your passions, your

abilities. Be you—bravely.

1. _____

2. _____

3. _____

4. _____

5. _____

6. _____

7. _____

Close friendships will result in misunderstandings and hurts, at times. You can either choose to forgive, or you can choose to be hurt and bitter.

Do you feel like forgiveness was
modeled in your childhood home?

*Friendships that stand the test of time
are those where both parties choose to
forgive when offenses and hurts come.*

8. _____

9. _____

10. _____

11. _____

12. _____

13. _____

14. _____

Throw yourself wholeheartedly into
developing roots and relationships here.
No one is guaranteed tomorrow.

What are you still holding onto—what hurt
or disappointment—that you need to forgive?

live today to the fullest.

15. _____

16. _____

17. _____

18. _____

19. _____

20. _____

21. _____

It's not easy and it means having hard conversations, but cultivating a heart of forgiveness will only deepen a friendship.

Think of two ways you were forgiven this week
(even when you didn't deserve it).

*At the end of my life, I want
to have used up everything I
was given—for others.*

22. _____

23. _____

24. _____

25. _____

26. _____

27. _____

28. _____

Deep friendships take time and investment.
They rarely happen overnight.

29. _____

30. _____

Does forgiveness flow freely in your closest relationships?

Close relationships are the result of much cultivation, time, and effort.

July

Choose love by believing the truth

Remember that your
struggles don't have
to define you.

1 spent years of my life disappointed with myself. I wasn't pretty enough, smart enough, funny enough, or eloquent enough. No matter what I did, I'd be frustrated with myself that it wasn't enough. I'd regularly think, *If only I were more this or that, then people would like me.*

What you believe determines how you live, and these beliefs held me back from many different things: from close friendships, to opportunities, to stepping outside my comfort zone. I lived in fear, guilt, insecurity, and shame, always feeling like I didn't measure up and was a perpetual failure. The past few years have been years of major transformation for me. It wasn't an overnight change but a gradual process of growing and healing. It hasn't been easy, but it has been so good.

1. _____

2. _____

3. _____

4. _____

5. _____

6. _____

7. _____

Your failings do not make you a failure.

Who or what do you tend to compare yourself to?

In what ways does that steal your joy?

*You are enough
exactly as you are.*

8. _____

9. _____

10. _____

11. _____

12. _____

13. _____

14. _____

Comparison is the thief of joy. Always.

What lies have you been told over the years that
make it difficult to feel fully accepted and loved?
How can you replace those lies with truth?

*You don't need to be thinner, more
organized, more fit, have a nicer wardrobe,
or get a better handle on your finances
to finally be enough. You are enough.*

15. _____

16. _____

17. _____

18. _____

19. _____

20. _____

21. _____

I'd rather be honest and authentic and
disappoint some people, than exhaust myself
trying to keep up a façade of perfection.

Do you tend to fall into the trap of people-pleasing?

Be done with living under the
bondage of being a people-pleaser.

22. _____

23. _____

24. _____

25. _____

26. _____

27. _____

28. _____

Start living with boldness and bravery.

29. _____

30. _____

31. _____

In what areas of your life do you long to live

with more boldness and bravery?

Want to have great friends?
Start by being the friend to
others you wish you had yourself.

August

Choose loving attitudes

Who is the only person
you can change?
Yourself.

Someone asked me the other day, "If you're feeling overwhelmed and discouraged by everything in your life, what is one of the most important things you can do to change your life?"

I thought of a lot of different practical things I could encourage someone to do, but at the heart of your success in anything in life is your attitude. If you have a can-do, creative, committed attitude, you'll go far in life. If you have a can't-do, won't-do, too hard, whiny attitude, you'll probably never go anywhere.

Change your attitude and you'll change your life. When the road ahead of you looks bleak, don't give up. When it feels impossible, keep going. When you want to throw in the towel, hang on. You never know what the struggles and difficulties you are going through now might be preparing you for in your future. Don't lose heart!

1. _____

2. _____

3. _____

4. _____

5. _____

6. _____

7. _____

If you choose to notice the good and praise-worthy things, it can transform your perspective. I dare you to try it and see if you can prove me wrong.

When in a difficult situation, do you tend to blame others 100%, or are you able to see the role you might have played as well?

Choose to be cheerful, flexible, and energetic as a mom today.

8. _____

9. _____

10. _____

11. _____

12. _____

13. _____

14. _____

You can choose your attitude.

Was there a time this week when your bad attitude
ended up ruining the whole day?

*Your attitude sets the
tone for your day—and
your life. So choose wisely.*

15. _____

16. _____

17. _____

18. _____

19. _____

20. _____

21. _____

Every day you wake up you have the
opportunity to choose your attitude.

Was there a time this week when you
consciously chose love over bitterness?

*Choose to be the victor,
not the victim.*

22. _____

23. _____

24. _____

25. _____

26. _____

27. _____

28. _____

You can inspire and motivate other people,
but ultimately you can only change you.

29. _____

30. _____

31. _____

How can you model a loving attitude to the
people you encounter in your daily life—
whether at home or in the workplace?

*True love requires sacrifices.
It costs us something,
but it's worth it!*

September

*Choose love
in authenticity*

There is beauty
in being our real
authentic selves.

*I*f you want to build close relationships, it starts

with being honest and authentic. A few years

ago, I had this revelation: If I wanted people to

love me for exactly who I was, I had to be exactly

who I was when I was with them.

I had to stop trying to please whoever I was with,

say what they'd want me to say, and walk on egg

shells for fear of offending them. Instead, I just

needed to be me—warts, shortcomings, and all.

This doesn't mean I need to air my dirty laundry

for everyone, nor does it mean I shouldn't be

considerate or use deference, but it does mean

that I am committed to being authentic and real

in my relationships.

1. _____

2. _____

3. _____

4. _____

5. _____

6. _____

7. _____

Don't compare your weaknesses to
someone else's strength.

Who do you secretly compare yourself to?

*What you believe
determines how you live.*

8. _____

9. _____

10. _____

11. _____

12. _____

13. _____

14. _____

You are not a misfit who isn't good enough—
you are beautiful in God's eyes.

Have you fully appreciated the fact that
God created you for a special purpose?

You were created
for a specific purpose.

15. _____

16. _____

17. _____

18. _____

19. _____

20. _____

21. _____

In God, you are whole, loved,
and 100% enough.

Name three gifts unique to you
that you can bless others with.

Recognize lies about yourself;
refuse to believe these lies,
and replace them with truth.

22. _____

23. _____

24. _____

25. _____

26. _____

27. _____

28. _____

Stop trying to be who you thought
you were "supposed" to be, and start
embracing who God has made you to be.

29. _____

30. _____

Is there a habit you need to break in your life in order to
help stop the habit of comparison (reading a certain blog,
checking Facebook constantly, etc.)?

*Stop wishing for other gifts and
talents and start owning the gifts
and talents God has given you.*

October

*Choose love in
the interruptions*

When you want to be
frustrated, choose love.
When your child asks you
the same thing again and
again, choose love.

*A*lways expect interruptions and delays in your day. This is not being negative; this is being realistic. Then, if they don't happen as often as you thought they would, you've been given the gift of more time and less frustration! Remember that your day won't ever go exactly as planned. You will make mistakes. Don't beat yourself up or wallow in guilt. Heap on the grace and remember that tomorrow is a new day!

1. _____

2. _____

3. _____

4. _____

5. _____

6. _____

7. _____

When your quiet is interrupted and you
want to be annoyed, choose love.

What hard thing happened this week when you were faced with the choice of reacting out of anger or frustration, or choosing love?

When your work relationships are strained, choose love.

8. _____

9. _____

10. _____

11. _____

12. _____

13. _____

14. _____

When your child needs you over
and over again, choose love.

How do you typically respond to interruptions?

How can you grow in this area?

When everything at home seems
to go wrong at the same time,
choose love.

15. _____

16. _____

17. _____

18. _____

19. _____

20. _____

21. _____

When you feel irritation rising up,
choose love.

What would help you begin to see interruptions
as ways to grow in patience?

When your child is making a big
deal about something you think
is unimportant, choose love.

22. _____

23. _____

24. _____

25. _____

26. _____

27. _____

28. _____

When your child demands more time
than you feel like you have, choose love.

29. _____

30. _____

31. _____

Did this month turn out as you had hoped and planned,
or was it something entirely different?

When your child decides
to test you, choose love.

November

Refuel so you can choose love

Taking time to replenish
your supply is not selfish;
it's actually enabling you
to be a better mom.

*I*t's time we quit using motherhood as a reason to no longer live to the fullest, no longer feed our soul and intellect, and no longer enjoy hobbies and relationships like we once did.

If you're constantly giving and giving and giving to others, if you're pouring and pouring and pouring into your family, if you're wringing yourself dry to meet the needs of others and you're never taking time to replenish, refresh, and refuel, it's no wonder you feel exhausted and spent!

1. _____

2. _____

3. _____

4. _____

5. _____

6. _____

7. _____

One of the best things you can do for
yourself and your kids is to take time
to refuel and refresh yourself.

Are you tempted to neglect investing in yourself,

even when it feels like your well has run dry?

*Stop and savor life. Make
time for things you love.*

8. _____

9. _____

10. _____

11. _____

12. _____

13. _____

14. _____

You will be more productive in the long-run
if you take a break now.

What are two simple things you can
include in your morning routine that will
immediately bring a bit of joy into your day?

A calmer, happier mom is one
who yells less and loves more.

15. _____

16. _____

17. _____

18. _____

19. _____

20. _____

21. _____

Think about what fills you up, what refreshes

you, or what makes you come alive.

Do you have a friend with whom you can refuel?
Read a book together, become walking or
running partners, establish a weekly coffee date.

Set aside some things you
think you have to do or must
do or feel obligated to do.

22. _____

23. _____

24. _____

25. _____

26. _____

27. _____

28. _____

Carve out some space to invest time in
some of the things you truly love.

29. _____

30. _____

Refueling doesn't have to be an hours-long process. If you had fifteen free minutes a few nights a week, what is one thing you would love to do that you know would refill your tank?

Sit down, smile, and just enjoy your children. Take time to laugh together, read a story, and share your heart.

December

Choose love amidst busyness

It's December! Determine today to have a peaceful, simple, memorable month, and not one filled with stress, busyness, and exhaustion.

We have Sundays set aside as a day off at our house. We go to church, come home, have a really simple lunch of some sort, and then have a quiet afternoon resting, reading, talking, playing a game, or engaging in other relaxing activities.

We don't blog, worry about business stuff or goals, and I often don't even turn on my phone or computer all day. It's a day we look forward to all week long! If you can't take a full day off, at least take half a day every week. I promise that you'll find you're more productive when you take time to recharge than if you just keep going and never stop to take a breath.

1. _____

2. _____

3. _____

4. _____

5. _____

6. _____

7. _____

Where does busyness get us? Often it just leads to exhaustion, frustration, stress, and burn-out.

Are you tempted into frenetic busyness
in the holiday season?

We live in a frantic, rushing world.
Busyness is a virtue: a badge of honor
we proudly wear. It shouldn't be.

8. _____

9. _____

10. _____

11. _____

12. _____

13. _____

14. _____

Making time for you—to breathe, to
refuel, to feel energized again—will make
you a calmer, happier mom.

Name the three most significant (and memorable) family traditions you have, and make those the top priority for the month of December.

We need to take time to breathe.

15. _____

16. _____

17. _____

18. _____

19. _____

20. _____

21. _____

We need to soak up the sunshine, the beauty,
the smells, the sounds, the wonder of life
teeming around us in all directions.

Are there traditions or habits that are not as
meaningful to your family that you could let go
for this year, to give some breathing room?

Stopping to smell the roses is not only
rejuvenating, it's imperative if you want
to lead a healthy, well-balanced life.

22. _____

23. _____

24. _____

25. _____

26. _____

27. _____

28. _____

Some of the deepest relationships often
blossom out of your willingness to take the
time to show someone you care about them.

29. _____

30. _____

31. _____

How can you set aside a little time for reflecting on the
blessings of this past year? Even a half hour this month
would be well worth your time.

*When no part of you
wants to choose love, do it
anyway. You won't regret it.*

A wife and homeschool mom of three, Crystal Paine is a bestselling author, business consultant, speaker, and the founder of MoneySavingMom.com. Started in 2007, Money Saving Mom® has since grown to be one of the top personal finance blogs on the web averaging over two million unique visitors per month. A New York Times bestselling author, her next book, *Money Making Mom: How Every Woman Can Earn More and Make a Difference* will release in November, 2015.

Crystal's mission is to help women from all walks of life discover the freedom that comes from living with intention, simplicity, and generosity. In addition to running her own business, she serves as a consultant to executives and business owners in the areas of brand development, online growth and social media strategy.

Crystal has contributed to articles in Woman's Day and All You magazines, appeared on Good Morning America and the 700 Club, and has been mentioned on The Today Show, National Public Radio, CNN, USA Weekend, Shop Smart magazine, Real Simple magazine, and numerous other local and national newspapers, radio, and television stations. She is also the author of the New York Times bestseller, *Say Goodbye To Survival Mode: 9 Simple Strategies to Stress Less, Sleep More, and Restore Your Passion for Life* and *The Money Saving Mom®'s Budget*.

Through her books and blog, Crystal seeks to encourage women and families to wisely steward their time, energy, and finances so that, ultimately, they might be able to bless and give more to those in their community and around the world.